I WANT TO BE HAPPY

I
WANT
TO BE
HAPPY

JOE R. BARNETT

PATHWAY PUBLISHING HOUSE, INC.

Grateful acknowledgement is made to the following for permission to reprint previously published material:

The Dallas Times Herald: Excerpt from "Life after death: survivors live in aftermath of terror of Grand Prairie slayings" by Ralph Frammolino, October 3, 1982. © 1982 by The Dallas Times Herald. Reprinted by permission.

Doubleday & Company: Excerpt from CELEBRATE YOU! by Faridi McFee, © 1982 by Doubleday & Company. Reprinted by permission.

Grosset & Dunlap: Excerpt from INSIDE LAS VEGAS by Mario Puzo, © 1976 by Grosset & Dunlap, New York. Reprinted by permission.

McGraw-Hill Book Company: Excerpt from IMAGINEERING by Michael LeBoeuf, © 1981 by McGraw-Hill Book Company, New York. Reprinted by permission.

William Morrow & Company, Inc.: Excerpt from GREAT BALLS OF FIRE: The Uncensored Story of Jerry Lee Lewis. © 1982 by Myra Lewis with Murray Silver. Reprinted by permission of William Morrow & Co.

The New York Times: Excerpt from "Private's Family Doubts He Defected," September 2, 1982. © 1982 by The New York Times. Reprinted by permission.

The New York Times: Excerpt from "Workaholism: Paying the Price," by Jane E. Brody, September 29, 1982. © 1982 by The New York Times. Reprinted by permission.

The New York Times: Excerpt from "After Hockey, Life Became Unbearable for Larry Mickey," September 8, 1982. © 1982 by The New York Times. Reprinted by permission.

People Weekly: Excerpt from "I was never prepared in life for such a horrendous thing to happen" by Suzanne Adelson, September 13, 1982. © 1982 by People Weekly. Reprinted by permission.

Alfred A. Knopf, Inc.: Excerpt from EDIE: AN AMERICAN BIOGRAPHY by Jean Stein with George Plimpton. © 1982 by Alfred A. Knopf. Reprinted by permission.

Reader's Digest: Excerpt from "Give Yourself a Life" by Hilton Gregory, November 1975. © 1975 by Reader's Digest. Reprinted by permission.

Reader's Digest: Excerpt from "You're Smarter Than You Think: by Dudley Lynch, November, 1978. © 1978 by Reader's Digest. Reprinted by permission.

Simon and Schuster: Excerpt from THE GAMESMAN: THE NEW CORPORATE LEADERS by Michael Maccoby. © 1976 by Simon and Schuster. Reprinted by permission.

U.S. News & World Report: Excerpt from "Secrets of Coping With Stress" interview with Dr. Hans Selye, March 21, 1977. © 1977 by U.S. News & World Report. Reprinted by permission.

Winston Press: THE ART OF AGING by Evelyn Mandel. © 1981 Evelyn Mandel. Reprinted with permission from Winston Press, Inc.

DEDICATION

To those who hurt.
Who want to be happy.
And are courageous
enough to try.

Contents

PART THREE
PROVEN PATHS

Preface

Every four-tenths of a second a newborn baby cries, its first sounds fashioned from the very breath of life.

Today, there are four-and-a-half billion of us.

People just like you and me.

And more arriving all the time.

People who live in more than 150 countries on this planet—and who speak who knows how many languages. Yet, despite our differences, and the conflicts which sometimes arise between us, we all share a common, universal longing—all saying . . .

I WANT TO BE HAPPY

People on the plains of Kenya and in the jungles of Brazil.

In Chicago, Singapore and Milan.

In London and Rio.

In Osaka, Oslo and Oshkosh.

All four-and-a-half billion of us—wanting to be happy.

"Not a single one but has at some time wept," said H. G. Wells.

But is happiness possible? Can this hope be satisfied? Or is happiness the Impossible Dream?

Good questions.

Questions which deserve honest answers.

I wouldn't be writing this book if I didn't believe there are answers.

But I also know answers aren't simple.

When I consider the pain I've seen in people's lives, I often think of the words of the poet, T. S. Eliot:

> Words strain
> Crack and sometimes break,
>   under the burden,
> Under the tension, slip, slide, perish
> Decay with imprecision, will not stay in place,
> Will not stay still.

Words can be easy. Cheap.

Words often prove inadequate and ineffective. Words can "slip, slide, perish."

That's why I haven't rushed in to offer some easy, smooth "Formula for Happiness."

Life brings pain.

You may be hurting deep down inside at this very moment.

Alone.

I wish I could offer you an easy escape from your hurt. But I can't. No one can.

My own deepest hurt comes when I encounter people in pain. It hurts *me* that I can't instantly eliminate their pain and make them happy. With the snap of a finger. Nothing would make me happier.

It isn't that easy. I know that.

But I am concerned about your hurts. I do want to help you find happiness. And I think I can.

I hope you will accept my interest (and my reluctance to offer advice) for what it is—a genuine concern.

Thanks for reading. And that's all I ask—that you read all the way to the end. Don't turn me off. And don't give up. Not yet anyway. Please give these suggestions—and happiness—a try.

I will try to remain aware of the fine line between words that "crack and sometimes break under the burden"—and words that can heal.

JOE R. BARNETT

PART ONE

Reaching
for
Happiness

1

Promises, Promises

Happiness! It's the world's most popular quest. Advertisers know this. "Happiness" is the bottom line of nearly every advertisement and TV commercial.

Buy our anti-headache formula, the makers of analgesics advertise. It will make the pain in your temples go away quickly.

Result? *Happiness!*

Buy our automobile, plead the car manufacturers' ads. It will make you the envy of your peers. It will get you there faster. It will get you there cheaper.

Result? *Happiness!*

Purchase a condominium from us, cry the developers. You will instantly enjoy the satisfaction of living in a world of comfort and elegant surroundings.

Result? *Happiness!*

Almost any consumer magazine today will carry a cover line announcing an article by a psychologist, minister, or "positive-thinking" expert, promising the secrets of happiness in a few easy-to-follow rules.

"Happiness—It's Only Natural" trumpets one magazine.

"Cure Yourself of Unhappiness" urges another.

Virtually every Sunday newspaper offers another definition, another formula.

Promises, promises!

And what is happiness?

Dr. Theodore Rubin, president of the American Institute for Psychoanalysis and a popular columnist, says happiness is feeling comfortable with yourself by accepting what you can and can't do.

Dr. Gerald Crary, a Los Angeles psychologist whose patients have included the rich and powerful, suggests that happiness is "fulfillment . . . living and working to your full potential."

Dr. Sidney Rosen, a New York City psychiatry professor, adds, "A sure sign is if you look forward to getting up in the morning."

We want to shout in response, "We know *that*! That's obvious. But what makes it happen? How can *I* achieve these ingredients of happiness?"

During the fall of 1982, the Canadian Broadcasting System provided an intriguing series of programs produced by Robert Blondin.

Blondin, a French-Canadian broadcaster, had just traveled to Sweden, the People's Republic of China, and many points in between. He interviewed more than 600 persons—of different colors, nations and languages.

He asked them one question—

"What is happiness?"

The answers were much the same everywhere.

Blondin saw a pattern developing. Money didn't seem terribly significant to happy people. And the happy-go-lucky people? Well, deep down they weren't as happy as people thought.

Blondin concluded that people are happy because of who they are—not because of what they have. Their happiness is strongly rooted in inner values, not outward circumstances.

They are happy because they are in control of themselves—and because they are willing to change.

They are happy because they can become totally absorbed—in their families, their friends, causes they believe in, and their work.

And they are happy because they see themselves as a part of something bigger than themselves.

After all his travels and interviews, Blondin reached the conclusion that truly happy people are happy because of their inner stability, not their outer security. No matter how much money they make, how big a house they live in, how well-known they are, or how much power they hold, people are happy only if they have peace *within*. Internal peace provides a foundation for life that may be buffeted by fierce storms—but seldom cracks.

But—unhappily—we have trouble accepting this. We repeatedly find ourselves chasing after dreams which turn brittle and break. We reach for images of wealth, pleasure, and influence that seem to dissolve as we grab for them. We can't shake free of the feeling that happiness in real life requires the trappings of pleasure, popularity, power and possessions. And that our inner

well-being is dependent upon our outward circumstances.

Don't misunderstand. It would be absurd to say
that our happiness is not affected by what happens to
us.

Each time I think of the great pain that Oklahoma
State Senator Phil Watson experienced, I get a lump in
my throat.

One morning in 1963 he kissed his wife and two-
year-old daughter good-bye—and never saw them
again. They, along with four students from the university where Phil taught, were killed when a train struck
their car.

And I think of the loss that Billie McDonald of
Irving, Texas, suffered when her husband of 42 years
recently died from cancer. They were in their "golden
years." Enjoying life. And each other. And suddenly he
was gone.

When such tragedies come, our happiness is dealt
a devastating blow. You can't go on as if nothing has
happened when you've just lost someone as close as a
wife, husband, child, or parent. You can't be jubilant
when you hurt. What happens to us is *not unimportant.*

But neither is it *all*-important. Happiness is not
completely at the mercy of "happenstance."

And what if things *are* going your way? What if you
do have the world at your feet—begging for your attention, ready to pay you big for your clout, your knowledge, or your skills? There is no assurance that it will
make you happy. And even if it seems to bring happi-

ness for the moment, you are terribly vulnerable if your happiness is tied only to those external ingredients.

And yet, in our pursuit of happiness we keep falling for the same illusion. Duped into believing "this is *the way*"—off we go, madly pursuing pleasure, popularity, power and possessions. The quartet that never honors its promises. In the right perspective, they all have their place. But when seen as the magic carpet to carry us to the Utopia of happiness, each stalls out and sputters to a disappointing stop.

2

What Is Your Happiness Level?

An old proverb says, "Happiness is a journey, not a destination."

Where are you on that journey?

Following are ten self-assessment exercises which will help you answer that question. Try each of the possible answers on "for size." It may help to close your eyes as you consider each question. Don't rush. Be certain that you are getting at your true feelings in this self-assessment of your happiness level.

Mark your answers, making a checkmark in the appropriate boxes.

1. When it comes to real friends, people I can count on when I need them, I have *(check only one box)*
1 □ None and never have had.
2 □ None at the moment.
3 □ One or two perhaps.

4 □ Several.
5 □ Many.

2. If one of my neighbors or someone else I know has a problem, I *(check only one box)*
1 □ Never get involved.
2 □ Rarely get involved.
3 □ Occasionally get involved.
4 □ Fairly often get involved.
5 □ Almost always get involved.

3. When I feel bored, I usually react to the feeling by *(check only one box)*
1 □ Just living with it.
2 □ Watching TV or reading.
3 □ Going shopping.
4 □ Calling a friend to talk or going to visit someone.
5 □ Looking for something new to do.

4. Thinking back over my life, I would say that I *(check only one box)*
1 □ Have been a total failure.
2 □ Made a wrong turn somewhere.
3 □ Have had a so-so life.
4 □ Have had things pretty good.
5 □ Am satisfied with things as they are.

5. If you would like to make some major changes in your life but haven't done so, which of the following reasons explains why? *(check only one box)*

1 □ I don't think it will make any difference.
2 □ I am afraid to make the changes I want.
3 □ My family or friends wouldn't approve.
4 □ I've got to make sure it is what I want.
5 □ I'm too busy at the moment doing other exciting
things.

6. When people criticize me, I usually *(check only one box)*
1 □ Withdraw, crushed and unhappy.
2 □ Criticize them right back.
3 □ Remember it and try to get even later.
4 □ Shrug it off.
5 □ Analyze it to see if it can help me but don't let it get
me down.

7. When I think about the future, I *(check only one box)*
1 □ Worry about it constantly.
2 □ Hope things won't get any worse.
3 □ Assume that things will be about the same.
4 □ Have some hope of a better life.
5 □ Am really optimistic about what is ahead.

8. In terms of controlling my life, I feel I have *(check only one box)*
1 □ Almost no control.
2 □ Control over the minor things.
3 □ Control perhaps half the time.

4 □ Some control most of the time.
5 □ Almost total control.

9. Check each statement below which you feel STRONGLY describes you:
□ I am a person you can depend on.
□ I smile and laugh a lot.
□ I find it easy to make people like me.
□ I work hard and am rewarded well for it.
□ When I need help, I find it is easy to ask for.
□ People often ask me for advice.

_____ Total number of checkmarks

10. Below is a list of 10 qualities which people admire in others. Place a checkmark by each of the qualities you feel accurately describes you.

□ Considerate   □ Energetic
□ Assertive   □ Cheerful
□ Creative   □ Responsible
□ Risk-taking   □ Intelligent
□ Productive   □ Friendly

_____ Total number of checkmarks

Now add up your score. On the first eight items, take the number beside each of the boxes you checked and write it on the corresponding line. For the last two items, take the number of checkmarks you made and write them on the lines provided. Then total your score.

1 _____
2 _____
3 _____
4 _____
5 _____
5 _____
6 _____
7 _____
8 _____
9 _____
10 _____

Total _____

Below is the scoring interpretation chart for the self-assessment exercise.

If your score falls between 8 and 24, you would appear to be experiencing a life with little variety. You are probably hurting and bored, and likely see little hope for a happier future.

If your score falls between 25 and 40, you probably experience occasional happiness, but it quickly disappears, leaving you unfulfilled and wanting more from life, friends, work and yourself.

If your score is between 41 and 52, you are living life on an even keel. You experience some moments of real happiness but not the kind that enables you to dream big dreams. You still lack a focus for your life which causes you to feel you have found your "life work" or a goal worth making a total commitment to.

If your score is 53 or over, congratulations. You have found happiness. And you share it with others.

If you scored low, don't give up! You aren't alone. Not by any means.

The George Gallup company, one of the world's great opinion-polling organizations, has discovered that at any given time, about *one in every three adult Americans* is going through a crisis, a period of unusual stress and inner conflict.

They are hurting, faced with difficult decisions and confusing options. Or they may see *no* options. They feel drained of resources, energies and self-confidence.

A year from now, if you went through this exercise again your score might be much different. Perhaps much higher. But what about now? What about tomorrow? What happens next?

You can give up, of course.

That's your option.

But if you can find it within yourself to take the first step, you may find that happiness isn't an impossible dream after all.

Solutions to unhappiness require some risk-taking. The risk of loving yourself, your family, your neighbors, even your enemies.

Only by opening up, by making yourself vulnerable can you love . . . and be loved.

"Love," as William Sloane Coffin, former chaplain at Yale, once said, "is an expression of (our) aliveness. Not to love is deadly."

I hope you will agree now to travel with me just a little further . . .

3

The Roads We Take

Someone described the wide-sky country of the Texas Panhandle where I live as mostly miles and miles of nothing but miles and miles. It is big country. Sliced by hundreds of roads. Side roads can be tricky. You can take a road thinking it will take you one place—and you end up somewhere else.

Life can be like that, too. Robert Frost knew this. He wrote,

> I shall be telling this with a sigh
> Somewhere ages and ages hence:
> Two roads diverged in a wood, and I—
> I took the one less traveled by,
> And that has made all the difference.

Each of us has confronted those diverging roads and debated the choice. At times we have made the choice by default—refusing to risk—either coming to a standstill at that point, or going the direction we were

27

pushed. At other times we have mustered the courage to choose—sometimes the choice was good; sometimes bad.

People have taken a lot of different roads hoping to find happiness. But somewhere along the way, many of them have taken a wrong turn.

Mary Bergman was into business for herself for the first time. By some standards she was doing great. Earning $100,000 or more a year. Writing contracts so fast she could scarcely keep up with them. Making contacts. Closing sales. But it wasn't working. Mary was rushing down roads that led nowhere. She wasn't happy.

"I couldn't get through a long weekend without alcohol, drugs, or both," she said. "I certainly had no self-respect. Total lack of self-esteem. I found myself turning for psychiatric help and I was in deep trouble."

There are a lot of roads we can take, but they don't all lead where we want them to go. And no matter which road we take, tragedy, disappointment and heartache can erupt in our lives like broken gas mains . . . sometimes through no fault of our own.

4

It's No Fairy Tale World

"You know when you get sick to your stomach? You know if you could throw up, you'd feel better? I never have thrown up, but sometimes I wish I could. Maybe I could get rid of this . . . I have actually [felt] so low that I literally had to tell myself to breathe. Breathe in. Breathe out . . It hurts. It hurts."

—Rosetta Ulrich

One of Eddie Ulrich's final projects was to plant a rose garden in his backyard in Lewisville, Texas. When his wife, Rosetta, walked into the bathroom one morning soon after, she found a message written in shaving cream on the mirror: "I love you." Sitting on the vanity were flowers. Roses.

The morning of August 9, 1982, Eddie left for his job and never came home. The telephone rang for Rosetta at work. Her daughter, Shari, 20, was calling. "Daddy's been shot," she blurted. After a frantic drive, the Ulrich family watched as paramedics walked out of Eddie's office, their faces cold as stone, their skills useless. An employee had gone berserk, firing a rifle and a pistol madly. Firing round after round at his fellow employees, most of whom he scarcely knew. Nine persons were hit. Eddie was one of the six who died.

For Rosetta Ulrich, words were suddenly slippery and cheap. "My friends come over, and I love them all," she said a few weeks later. "But when they leave, I know they can go home to their family, their husband or their wife and whatever, and I'm . . . [Oh] . . . I miss him."

"My mother finally took Edie out of Manhattan State Hospital and brought her back to the ranch in the late fall of 1968. She couldn't walk. She'd just fall over. . . . The doctor did a dye test of some sort and it showed the blood wasn't reaching certain parts of the brain; they said that in the X-ray pictures it looked like Swiss cheese. She couldn't talk! . . . Every day it would be a little better. You could see how desperate it was when you looked into her eyes and you could see how hard she was trying to reach you."

—Jonathan Sedgwick

Jonathan Sedgwick is one of 250 persons interviewed and quoted by Jean Stein in her best-selling book *Edie*, the story of Edie Sedgwick's search for happiness. Edie was Jonathan's sister.

Edie sped through the decade of the 1960s like a comet, searching, sampling and often trampling life. She starred in an underground film classic, *Ciao! Manhattan,* and she knew dozens of luminaries of the times from coast to coast. But the world still didn't revolve fast enough for her. She tried to rush it along with drugs: speed, heroin and coke.

Edie found variety, and notoriety. But not much happiness. This waifish blond beauty died of a drug overdose in 1971. At age 28.

"I didn't know anything. I had nothing to contribute. All I'd ever done was work."
—Dr. X

He was a doctor . . . a highly successful one by most standards. He had completed two medical residency programs and received board certification in both specialties. Now, at age 33, this New York physician was wealthy, respected, in demand. And, in his words, a "dud."

He told writer Jane E. Brody of going on a camping trip with his wife and an experienced group of campers. Suddenly, he was overwhelmed with the emptiness of his life. Others in the group were experiencing the richness of life—going to plays and museums, reading good books, making friends, and enjoying a lot of things with those friends.

But all he knew was medicine. All he could talk about was being a doctor. A workaholic, he had come to realize that the bottom line of his relentless personal pursuit was deep melancholy and a sense of failure. Not failure as a doctor. But failure as a human being.

———————

"It is eerie to lie in an ambush position with 96 rounds of live ammo in your magazine pouches at 3 A.M. and listen to the voice of a Communist woman, which is quivering with hate. Hate for the U.S. and the Republic of Korea. I almost got killed twice two patrols ago. Warrior Base is a God-forsaken, wretched place . . . If it isn't boiling, it's raining, and when it's raining it pours."
—Pfc. Joseph T. White

Not long after he wrote those words, Pfc. Joseph T. White may have decided not to listen any longer to the voice of hate blaring across the Demilitarized Zone, that "no man's land" separating North and South Korea. In late August, 1982, the 20-year-old soldier disappeared from his post. A North Korean announcement said White had crossed the demarcation line and requested political asylum.

The news was shattering to his parents. His father's and mother's faces were etched with despair as they talked with reporters outside their working-class row house on St. Louis' South Side. "My son did not cross that line," insisted Kathleen White. "He loved this country and he loved that uniform and everything about it. Joey was nothing but gung-ho Army . . ."

The details of Private White's disappearance are

still too complex to untangle. But for his mother and father, the pain of that day will never be forgotten. Pain that hit like a bullet. And left a bullet's scar.

————————

"I wonder if he had just been normal, if he hadn't been a hockey player or an athlete. They're brought up to be special. 'Hey, look at me.' It's easy for athletes—the girls all over you, you're the big star. But it's not easy once they take their skates off. It's a rude awakening."

—Lynda Mickey

Larry Mickey grew up living and breathing hockey in his home town of Ponoka, in the western Canadian province of Alberta. When the ice rinks in town were too crowded, Larry and his friends played on the packed snow in the street.

At 5 feet, 11 inches and 180 pounds, the hard-charging Mickey put body and soul into playing professional hockey. But he was never more than average. Seven teams in the National Hockey League used his body and his determination for the dirty jobs in hockey—penalty killer, digger, enforcer. For 12 seasons. The injuries grew more and more serious. Broken legs. Broken ankles.

In 1975 there was no new contract to sign. But Larry wouldn't quit. He began coaching in the minors. He ran hockey schools. He refereed junior hockey. And he played with the Niagara Falls Old-Stars, a group of former NHL players. He coached a team in Virginia that ran out of funds. He paid the players himself . . . and he played again. But finally, the inevitable forced his hand. He agreed to call it quits.

He took a job as a salesman and tried to settle down with his family in a suburb of Buffalo. But he was miserable away from the rink. "I asked him many times if he was happy," his wife, Lynda, recalled. "I couldn't see any happiness in him. All these years we spent together, we didn't really talk."

One day in mid-July, 1982, Larry tried unsuccessfully to kill himself, taking a drug overdose and leaving his car running in his garage. Six days later a bailiff served him with divorce papers. Lynda was tired of the turmoil, of all the talk of killing himself when she thought he was bluffing. The following morning, at age 38, Larry left no doubts.

The coroner's verdict: suicide by carbon monoxide poisoning.

I wanted them dead. It was an evil thought but a powerful one, and I knew if I thought it hard enough, it would happen."
                                        —Doris Gwendolyn Tate

At the time she was murdered by Charles Manson's homicidal "family," Sharon Tate was eight-and-a-half months pregnant. Her killers ignored her cries to spare her baby's life. They held the 26-year-old actress down and brutally stabbed her—and her baby—to death.

When word of the senseless murder reached Sharon's mother, Doris Gwendolyn Tate, and her father,

Paul Tate, a paralyzing shock ensued, followed by feelings of rage and the desire for revenge. Tate launched his own search for the killers, haunting hippie bars in Hollywood, seeking information, watching for signs of suspicious characters. "He was frustrated and mad at the same time, and felt so helpless. And I could barely function, even though I had other children," Gwen Tate recalled 13 years later.

Today, each time one of the Manson gang comes up for parole, Gwen Tate joins efforts by such groups as Parents of Murdered Children in soliciting signatures for petitions opposing the release. The desire for revenge has cooled, she says. Now, she sees her determination to keep the Manson murderers away from society forever as an "act of principle." But the events of August 9, 1969, are forever seared in her memory. Every day is a trial, she says. Every day is a challenge. Just to live, to breathe. To find a little happiness to mix with her lingering sorrow.

This is no "Fairy Tale" world we live in. Real-people stories seldom have a "they lived happily ever after" ending. Dreams often crumble.

Little girls playing with dolls, grow into big girls, maybe leading cheers. And cheerleaders grow into women, often facing a life of dishes, diapers, and divorce. Or perhaps death and disaster like those that struck Rosetta Ulrich and Gwen Tate.

Little boys playing astronaut may grow into sports heroes with moments of grandeur. But those sports heroes become grown men, often facing family problems, business frustrations, financial failure and the feelings of futility which come with blunt realities like those that confronted Private White's father and Larry Mickey.

Or perhaps everything *does* go according to plan. The cheerleader grows up to marry prestige and adventure, or to achieve it on her own. And the sports hero grows up and achieves success and fortune. Even then, the bottom line can turn out like that of Jane Brody's workaholic physician. Emptiness. Absence of meaning. Unhappiness. It eats into us like acid.

It's so easy to look for happiness in the wrong places.

5

Seeking Happiness in . . . Possessions, Popularity, Pleasure, Power

I once heard a well-known and highly-respected speaker say, "We all seek happiness in one of four things—or in some combination of them: possessions, popularity, pleasure, or power."

At the time, I doubted that assessment. But with additional observation I have concluded he was very close to accurate.

These four items—and our pursuit of happiness through them—deserve closer observation.

THE PURSUIT OF POSSESSIONS

In one of Charles Schulz's *Peanuts* cartoons, Linus is talking to Charlie Brown. "I'd like to make a lot of money, but I'd hate to be a snob," he says, looking very earnest.

He continues: "I've given this a lot of thought."

"So what have you decided?" asks Charlie Brown.

"So I've decided to be a very rich and famous

person who doesn't really care about money and who is very humble but who still makes a lot of money and is very famous, but is very humble and rich and famous."

Charlie Brown, with a blank stare responds, "Good luck!"

It is easy to be confused about possessions. About getting and having and keeping and, in Linus' words, still being able to be humble, and avoid being a snob.

We are bombarded by advertisements, radio and television commercials, salespeople, and free samples. And there is constant peer pressure to increase our "getting"—to keep buying, consuming, and accumulating far beyond basic needs.

Possessions alone can't make us happy. We know that. But, for some unexplainable reason, we continue scratching and clawing to get more . . . and more . . . and more. Financial success is our number one goal—our "god."

The Bible cautions against an easy truce with prosperity:

> But those who desire to be rich fall into temptation, into a snare, into many senseless and hurtful desires that plunge men into ruin and destruction. For the love of money is the root of all evils; it is through this craving that some have wandered away from the faith and pierced their hearts with many pangs *(1 Timothy 6:9,10).*

Jesus once said, "Take heed, and beware of all covetousness; for a man's life does not consist in the abundance of his possessions" (Luke 12:15).

Then he told a story about a rich farmer. A man whose harvest was so abundant his barns wouldn't hold it all. There was only one thing to do. Build new barns. Bigger ones. And he had the money to do it.

Proudly he said, "Lucky man! You have all the good things you need for many years. Take life easy, eat, drink and enjoy yourself!" (Luke 12:19, Today's English Version).

He had arrived. He was successful. And surely, happy. Nothing bad could happen now. But listen to the end of the story:

> God said to him, "Fool! This night your soul is required of you; and the things you have prepared, whose will they be?" *(Luke 12:20)*.

Does this mean financial success is wrong? That poverty and holiness are one and the same? Not at all! The Bible teaches that our blessings are from God, and should be received with thanksgiving.

There is nothing wrong with possessions. With financial success. The danger is in being *consumed by a passion for getting.*

We *can* pay too high a price for financial success.

We are paying too high a price when we let it corrupt us.

When we compromise our morals, violate our ethics, and distort our sense of values we've paid too much. We may get what we're after. But eventually the investment will seem shabby and shallow. And life deep down will be empty—and unhappy.

We are paying too high a price when things become more important than people.

When a visitor from India approached the Times Square subway station he was astounded by what he saw: people with attache cases wildly pushing and shoving each other. "Is there a devil after them?" he asked.

"No," someone replied, "there is a dollar in front of them." Success is tarnished by misplaced priorities.

We have the capacity to rise above the mundane, earthly levels of life. We have an instinct for the Eternal. And we can never be satisfied until we attach to it. In a sentence, ". . . God gave us eternal life, and this life is in his Son" (1 John 5:11). This unique quality must never be left out of our definition of success.

THE PURSUIT OF POPULARITY

One of the more glamorous roads in the pursuit of happiness is popularity. The glitter of fame and prestige is alluring. For many, the applause of the crowd appears to be the magic carpet to the pinnacle of happiness.

Steve Kelly, Denver's well-known disk-jockey, knows about popularity. He has it. He described himself as "the funny guy on the radio. The big popular, fun-loving, happy-go-lucky, rebel of the air waves."

But then there came that time every day when he went off the air. Went home. What then?

"I wasn't the same person on the air as off the air," he said. "And I kept saying to myself, you've got it made. You have everything you could ask for. Recognition and popularity and all this stuff."

But Steve wasn't happy.

"Something wasn't there," he said. "That's sure an empty feeling, you know, when you're trying to be happy, you want so desperately to be happy. And yet you're lonely. And I didn't know how not to be lonely."

Those who frantically seek popularity will often go to any lengths to get it. Often the path is dangerous, dead-ending in pain and disappointment.

Nancy Jane Short, a Tennessee teen-ager, is fighting her way back from the edge of oblivion. She tried it all—drugs, illicit sex, alcohol. She knows what it's like to be arrested. Jailed. A horrible traffic accident left her badly broken. At the age of 18, Nancy Jane had lived the equivalent of three lives—all of them crammed with unhappiness.

She said:

"I slept with boys during junior high so that I'd be accepted.

"I tried drugs in high school—so that I'd be accepted.

"I have always wanted to be popular. I guess that's why I had my first sex at 13. Even now, I don't have a lot of friends. I admit I'm naive. I always thought everyone had my best interest at heart. Boy, was I wrong!"

Popularity depends on people. But people are not always dependable. They sometimes *use* others—until they don't need them anymore. Popularity can be fleeting.

Remember Jerry Lee Lewis? He went to England for a six-week concert tour in the spring of 1958. He was the self-acknowledged king of rock and roll. Just a year before, Jerry had cut a record that sold in the millions. He made smash appearances on "The Steve Allen Show" and Dick Clark's "American Bandstand." He was making $10,000 a day.

Then came disaster.

In London, the British press learned that Lewis's young companion on the tour was actually Myra Lewis, the singer's third wife. Reporters quickly dug out the facts that she was only 13-years-old—and that she was his cousin. And they learned that Lewis was not yet divorced from his second wife.

His fans abandoned him.

Newspaper headlines screamed for Lewis to go home.

His concerts were interrupted with taunts and sneers.

The House of Commons debated the issue of Jerry Lee Lewis, and the Home Office finally started extradition procedures. The tour was cancelled. And so was the popularity of Jerry Lee Lewis. In her book *Great Balls of Fire,* Myra Lewis wrote:

Hardly two years had elapsed since the un-
known itinerant piano player had first stepped
into a studio, then ascended in June of 1957
with one of the biggest-selling singles in pop
music history. When next June appeared on
the calendar, Jerry's star had dropped below
the horizon. The good ol' days, of which there
were exactly 569, were over.

Popularity isn't a strong foundation upon which to
build a life. And, like drugs, it takes more and more—
ever-increasing doses—to provide the same "high."

Deep down, what we are all looking for—whether
Marilyn Monroe, Jerry Lee Lewis, Steve Kelly, or you and
me—are relationships which give us a sense of belong-
ing. Relationships which thrive only in an atmosphere of
openness, honesty and trust.

THE PURSUIT OF PLEASURE

In his book, *Inside Las Vegas,* Mario Puzo has a
photo of a huge billboard out in the Nevada desert with
just five words on it: "Las Vegas—24 hour entertain-
ment."

Twenty-four-hour pleasure.

Puzo writes,

Today Las Vegas is perhaps the best-known
city in the entire world. A newspaper story
datelined Las Vegas will immediately get

space in any newspaper on the globe. Travel through the centers of civilization in Europe and ask any taxi driver or hotel waiter a question about Las Vegas and you will have his immediate attention. Go East to Japan and Hong Kong and the people there will talk to you about Las Vegas and how they hope one day to go there.

But does Las Vegas deliver? Does it produce the happiness it promises?

Standing for a few minutes in Las Vegas' busy airport provides the answer. First, watch the arriving passengers—loud, boisterous, excited. Eager to taste the offerings of the Pleasure Capital of the World. And then, for contrast, watch the people who are leaving.

The difference is incredible. Revealing.

The faces of those who are leaving are often drawn and distant. There are unmistakable signs of defeat, discomfort and disappointment. Whatever pleasures they enjoyed while there aren't even durable enough to last until they can get out of town.

Many have told of the emptiness waiting at the end of their all-consuming quest for pleasure. Rob's story sticks in my mind.

"My extra marital affairs began while I was in college," he confided. "It seemed during this time that sex was like an addiction. I liked what I was doing, but at the same time after being with a woman, sometimes I would get sick . . . because I really knew it was wrong. I loved my wife. Yet at the same time I could not give up sex. It was like another hill to conquer."

There has never been a more intense pleasure-seeker than King Solomon. Whatever he wanted, he got. If he thought it would bring him happiness, he laid down the money and took it.

Here is a description of his extravagance:

> I made great works; I built houses and planted vineyards for myself; I made myself gardens and parks, and planted in them all kinds of fruit trees. I made myself pools from which to water the forest of growing trees. I bought male and female slaves, and had slaves who were born in my house; I had also great possessions of herds and flocks, more than any who had been before me in Jerusalem. I also gathered for myself silver and gold and the treasure of kings and provinces; I got singers, both men and women, and many concubines, man's delight.

> So I became great and surpassed all who were before me in Jerusalem; also my wisdom remained with me. And whatever my eyes desired I did not keep from them; I kept my heart from no pleasure. . . *(Ecclesiastes 2:4-10)*.

King Solomon was easily a billionaire. He spent 13 years building himself a house, using 70,000 men to carry materials, 80,000 to hew stone and 3,300 managers to oversee the construction. He had so many horses that he needed 40,000 stalls and 12,000 horsemen. And he was never lacking for company, female or otherwise.

When the Queen of Sheba, who was certainly no amateur in the pursuit of pleasure, came for a visit, she took one look at Solomon's opulent lifestyle—and fainted.

Staggering success. Mountains of money. And he did it with a flair that has never been matched. Man, that's living!

But wait! Was he happy?

Let *him* answer!

Then I considered all that my hands had done and the toil I had spent in doing it, and behold, all was vanity and a striving after wind, and there was nothing to be gained under the sun *(Ecclesiastes 2:11).*

Lasting happiness doesn't come from sensual pleasure. Life is meant for more noble investments. How, then, can you deal with the temptation to grab for such pleasures?

First, you can resist. Simple as that. Run away. Understanding your own weaknesses, you can head the other direction when you recognize an approaching temptation. There are some windows in your life which should be boarded up. That takes strength.

Second, you can cultivate the right kind of relationships. Martin Luther said temptation should not be faced alone. He suggested that we seek the company of supportive, understanding people. Each temptation you face has been experienced by others. You can find strength in sharing with them.

Third, you can resolve to win over temptation. There is a tradition that Augustine was approached by a former mistress shortly after his conversion to Christianity. He turned and walked away. The surprised woman cried out, "Augustine, it is I."

He replied, "Yes, but it is not I." There was a new Augustine. He had decided. And he won.

THE PURSUIT OF POWER

"Troubled bank exec killed in Milan fall," the newspaper headline blared. The article noted that this was the third official of an Italian bank who had apparently committed suicide in less than four months.

The bank had collapsed. And these officials who, just a short time before, had been some of Italy's most powerful financial moguls now found themselves accused, ostracized, and stripped of influence. These top executives couldn't live with that burden. Two leaped to their deaths, and the third was found hanging from scaffolding under London's Blackfriars Bridge.

Power—like possessions, popularity and pleasure—promises more happiness than it can deliver. In recent years the shelves in America's book stores have bulged with books urging us to *Look Out for No. 1, Pull Your Own Strings, Win Through Intimidation*—in general, to get power at any cost and ruthlessly use it for personal advantage. Others, however, have been questioning the high costs of power.

Power often corrupts. And it frequently detours the development of meaningful relationships. Such was Michael Maccoby's conclusion in *The Gamesman.* He interviewed 250 business managers from 12 major American companies. He learned the people with power isolate themselves—in their corporate offices, homes and hotel rooms.

"What happens to a person who spends too much time living in enclaves, hotels, jet planes, and corporate offices?" he asks. His answer: they withdraw from the capacity to feel, to enjoy, to be happy. He writes:

> When I get into this kind of life, I also escape into myself, away from the machinelike rhythms, antiseptic smells, Muzak, and tasteless rooms; it takes days to feel alive again, and for many executives, this atmosphere of the mechanical womb reinforces the detachment of their every day lives.

For years I've kept a clipping in my desk drawer about a group of the world's most successful financiers. Powerful men. In 1923 they met at the Edgewater Beach Hotel in Chicago. Present were the president of the nation's largest independent steel company, the president of the New York Stock Exchange, a member of the President's cabinet, the most powerful man on Wall Street, the president of the Bank of International Settlements and the head of the world's greatest monopoly. Combined, these men controlled more wealth than the United States Treasury.

Twenty-five years later a reporter traced the lives of these powerful men. This is what he found:

The president of the largest independent steel company, Charles Schwab, lived on borrowed money the last five years of his life and died broke.

The president of the largest utility company, Samuel Insull, died broke and in disgrace.

The president of the New York Stock Exchange, Richard Whitney, had gone to prison.

The member of the President's cabinet, Albert Fall, had been pardoned from prison so he could die at home.

The greatest investor on Wall Street, Jesse Livermore, committed suicide.

And so did the head of the world's greatest monopoly, Ivan Krueger.

Happiness in power? No. It isn't enough.

PART TWO

Taking Control

6

The One Place You Are in Control

For baseball fans, October means the Series, that yearly explosion of excitement that determines the champion of major league baseball. It's unforgettable, no matter who wins.

The 1982 National League playoffs and the World Series excited me more than usual—because of Darrell Porter, catcher for the Saint Louis Cardinals.

The intense, somber-faced Mr. Porter gave us all the excitement we could handle, winning the Series' Most Valuable Player award. He pounded out extra-base hits in the clutch, and threw out the opponent's runners as they tried to steal bases. He was a picture of determination, of quiet courage—a man with a mission, a portrait of self-control, a leader.

What a change!

Darrell Ray Porter had been in the World Series before. In the 1980 Series he played five games for the Kansas City Royals—and says he has almost no memory of those games. He batted 17 times, got two hits, scored one run—*and can recall none of it*. That time in his life is virtually blank. In the autumn of 1980, Porter's life was unraveling.

He had arrived in the heady, pressurized ranks of major league baseball at the tender age of 19, straight out of high school. He could have starred for any college or university in three sports—baseball, football or basketball. He was a gifted, versatile athlete. But he bypassed college to play baseball. To make lots of money.

Back home in Oklahoma City, his high school buddies bragged about "Ol' Darrell." Darrell, they said, could do it all. Drugs. Alcohol. The World Series. What they didn't know was that their friend Darrell was coming apart. Self-destructing. "I was a miserable human being," Darrell says.

But at that moment, when prospects were bleakest, Darrell Porter, drug addict, took command. He said, "Whoaaa." He admitted to himself that he had taken a wrong turn and was barreling down the wrong road. Realizing how close he was to the edge of oblivion, he had himself admitted to The Meadows, a drug treatment center in Arizona. And he started the long road back.

It wasn't easy. "I'll tell you what, you don't get better overnight," he says. "I've struggled ever since."

It's been a successful struggle. A warm and inspiring story. For those who find themselves in Darrell Porter's shoes—confused, in the pits, dangerously close to destruction—here is a powerful lesson in courage. Self-control.

The moral of Darrell Porter's successful comeback

as a baseball player and as a human being is this: If you want to conquer your weaknesses, if you want to find meaning, if you want to be happy—you have to start somewhere. And there's really only one place to start.

With yourself.

Because that's the only place where you are really in control!

You Can't Control Other People

The late Martha Mitchell, one of the victims of Watergate, lived the latter part of her life a miserable woman.

In 1965, she was in a reflective mood as she met with author Max Gunther and two of his editors in New York.

"There was a time," she said, "when I had the world on a leash. I had everything I wanted, and I also had a feeling of control. I felt I was in control of my life. I thought, 'As long as I'm careful, nothing can slip away from me now.' Well, the feeling was false. It all slipped away. There were precautions I could have taken, things I could have done, if only I hadn't felt so strong and confident . . ."

Among other things, Martha Mitchell learned she couldn't control people.

She couldn't control the Watergate burglars, who triggered the events which brought Mrs. Mitchell, and so many others, down.

She couldn't control President Nixon.

She couldn't control her husband, John, the Attorney General.

She couldn't control the Washington socialites who avoided her after the Watergate scandal broke.

She couldn't control the news people who hounded her.

She couldn't control the curious who rudely invaded her privacy.

"Life is slippery like a piece of soap" she said. "If you think you have a good grip on it, you are wrong."

Slippery, for sure. Because you can't control people. People can be fickle. Cruel and untrustworthy. People can mistreat you. They don't always act fairly and responsibly. Not always with integrity.

You can love people or hate them. Build them up or cut them down. Help them or hurt them. But you can't control them.

You Can't Always Control Circumstances

Calamities do come.

I was reminded of this as I listened to Steve Neff tell of the loss of his three-month-old son to crib death. There was futility, and helplessness in Steve's voice as he said, "I just woke up that morning and I knew something was wrong. Of course, I couldn't do anything. He was dead."

When tragedies like this occur it is easy to assume guilt. Paralyzed with the "what if's?" and "if only's." It's hard to reconcile our tragedies with who we thought we were. Steve had bought into the American view of the "rugged male individualist." Strong. Self-sufficient. Ready to tackle any challenge, any adversary—and come out a winner. That self-image was shattered by the death of his baby. For months Steve struggled with a sense of guilt, of bungled responsibility.

But what could he have done to prevent the death of his child?

Nothing. Nothing at all.

I can't help but think of a famous Bible personality when I think of uncontrollable circumstances. Remember Job?

> There was a man in the land of Uz, whose name was Job; and that man was blameless and upright, one who feared God and turned away from evil. There were born to him seven sons and three daughters. He had seven thousand sheep, three thousand camels, five hundred yoke of oxen, and five hundred she-asses, and very many servants; so that this man was the greatest of all the people of the east *(Job 1:1-3)*.

Sounds good so far. But read the whole story and you discover incredible suffering.

Job lost all his possessions.

All ten of his children were killed by a tornado.

He lost his health and suffered horrible pain.

His friends deserted him.

Even his wife turned against him.

By any measurement, Job didn't deserve what happened to him.

In his book *Imagineering,* Michael LeBoeuf says,

"Despite the greatest efforts of governments, clergy-men, judges and the like, life isn't fair and never will be ... I don't mean this to be a cynical look at life but rather an accurate portrayal of the way things are ... the list of injustices in this world is infinite."

Some people refer to it as "bad luck." Others talk about Murphy's Law: "If anything can go wrong, it will." And one wit insisted, "Murphy was an optimist."

And there are other circumstances beyond our control. In periods of business recession hundreds of people lose their jobs. Others have pledged their lives to a corporation, believing that loyalty and hard work will pay off with a better job, higher pay, more respon-sibility, increased opportunity.

But in the end only a few employees of any corpo-ration can experience "the view at the top." The rest face the disappointment of not making it.

Some of these "also-rans" successfully adjust—finding new goals, new interests, new ways to use their talents and enjoy life. And some do not.

It's sometimes referred to as the "just world" the-ory—the idea that we all get what we deserve. If we are "good"—if we do what is right and honorable—our "luck" will be good. Our rewards will be certain.

I've mentioned those uncontrollable job situations, and Steve Neff, and Job to emphasize that the "just world" theory leaks badly. You don't always get what you deserve. "Luck" can be bad as well as good. You can't totally control your circumstances. You may suffer poverty, illness, loss of a loved one, or divorce—maybe through no fault of your own. You may be unfairly accused, criticized, belittled.

The inability to control *people* and *circumstances* is part of "the human condition."

But . . .

You Can Control You

Oh, you may have habits that are haunting you. You may have tried self-control—and failed. But don't give up.

Self-control doesn't come easily. It takes time. And patience. Courage. Determination. There are choices to be made—forks in the road.

Clarence Macartney told of a man sitting alone in a hotel room far away from home. He was struggling. About to ring for room service and place an order which would entrench him more deeply in a destructive habit.

He said to himself, "This is your hour. If you yield to this temptation now it will destroy you. If you conquer it now, you are its master forever." He took control. And won. That's the only way to take control. *Self*-control.

It's what Job did. He couldn't control those cruel circumstances. By any reasonable expectation, he would have been justified in giving up. No one would have much blamed him if he had cursed God, life, and the injustice of it all—and retreated into permanent unhappiness and self-pity.

But he didn't. After wrestling with periods of

shock, despair, nostalgia, anger, resentment and self-justification, Job's deep faith and immense courage won. He said, "Naked I came from my mother's womb, and naked shall I return; the Lord gave, and the Lord has taken away; blessed be the name of the Lord" (Job 1:21).

Don't hang your happiness on what others do or don't do. It's your life. You have to live it. Call the shots. Choose the roads you will travel.

Don't allow either circumstances or other people to control your sleep habits, your health, your goals, your future—your happiness. Your happiness begins with you.

That's not easy advice. Have you been mistreated? Probably. You may be able to point to someone who did a mean, nasty thing to you. But that won't change anything. You just have to be bigger than that person . . . if you want to be happy.

Don't waste time, energy, and health on hate. S. I. McMillen, in *None of These Diseases,* wrote:

> The moment I start hating a man, I become his slave. I can't enjoy my work any more because he even controls my thoughts. My resentments produce too many stress hormones in my body and I become fatigued after only a few hours of work. The work I formerly enjoyed is now drudgery. Even vacations cease to give me pleasure.
>
> The man I hate hounds me wherever I go. I can't escape his tyrannical grasp on my

mind. When the waiter serves me porterhouse steak with French fries, asparagus, crisp salad, and strawberry shortcake smothered with ice cream, it might as well be stale bread and water. My teeth chew the food and I swallow it, but the man I hate will not permit me to enjoy it.

The man I hate may be miles from my bedroom; but more cruel than any slave driver, he whips my thoughts into such a frenzy that my innerspring mattress becomes a rack of torture . . . I really must acknowledge the fact that I am a slave to every man on whom I pour the vials of my wrath.

And don't hang your self-esteem on circumstances. Your circumstances may be lousy. Don't let that erode your self-image. Your worth doesn't vary with circumstances. You are a beautiful, wonderful, valuable, important human being.

Take control of you!

7

Begin

It's easy for me to *talk* about these things.

But what about a plan of action? Where do you go from here? What do you do now?

Begin!

That's all. Just begin. The longest journey begins with a single step. You can't take the quantum leap from where you are to a Magic Kingdom of perfection, accomplishment and happiness.

But you can take the first step.

Don't berate yourself because you can't do it all right now. Rome wasn't built in a day.

Eric Severeid, long-time news commentator, said at his retirement that he had written more than 2,000 scripts for his on-the-air appearances. He said if he had known when he wrote the first one that he would have to write another 2,000 he probably would never have started. But because he only wrote one at a time, he was never faced with the awesome task of writing that mountain of scripts.

62

At this point your life may seem very imcomplete. It may seem impossible to be all you want to be—to possess all the admirable qualities you desire. You want wholeness and balance and
> patience,
> enthusiasm,
> courage,
> vision,
> inspiration,
> faith,
> sensitivity,
> determination,
> optimism,
> confidence,
> goodness,
> unselfishness,
> compassion,
> creativity,
> goodwill,
> love,
> peace,
> and, of course, happiness.

I believe you can have all these things. But you'll have to take it one step at a time.

And here is the first step:

Affirm the Wonderful You

An authority on the inner workings of our emotional and mental development has written, "Affirmations are statements of truth, which when spoken with

conviction, are a strong vibratory force that destroys
negative thoughts, wrongful habits, and harmful mental
patterns which cause ill health, anxiety and fear. Affirmations, repeated continually with concentration, stimulate and direct the flow of life energy to bring about
physical, mental and spirutal healing . . ."

In *Celebrate You!,* Faridi McFree says, ". . . Affirmations will act as catalysts to help heal the emotions, and
your own . . . abilities will be developed and unblocked,
enabling you to change your negative thought patterns
and create positive action in your life."

I want you to make some affirmations.

It is important for you to be physically and men-
tally relaxed when you are "seeding" affirmative
thoughts in your mind. Sit in a comfortable chair. Close
your eyes. Breathe deeply. Deliberately relax the mus-
cles in your shoulders, your neck, your hips, your legs,
your feet.

First, read these affirmations silently. Think about
each one. Let it sink in deeply. Don't rush. Feel its
warmth and power.

Then go back to the top of the list. This time read
each one out loud. Repeat the ones you especially like
several times. And in between each one, wait a few
moments. Don't rush. Let your mind slowly absorb it.

Then return to the top of the list one more time.
This time through, speak loudly. Shout if you wish. Make
these affirmations about yourself. You are a marvelous
person!

Ready? Let's begin.

Affirmation No. 1: I AM A UNIQUE AND WONDERFUL PERSON, A CHILD OF GOD.

Affirmation No. 2: INSIDE, I AM STRONG AND HEALTHY.

Affirmation No. 3: TODAY, I WILL BE KIND AND THOUGHTFUL REGARDLESS OF THE ACTIONS OF OTHERS.

Affirmation No. 4: TODAY I WILL BE CHEERFUL AND POSITIVE.

Affirmation No. 5: TODAY I WILL BE OPEN TO CHANGE, GROWTH AND NEW OP-PORTUNITY.

Affirmation No. 6: I AM A PERSON OF GREAT VALUE AND WORTH.

Affirmation No. 7: GOD LOVES ME AND TODAY I WILL LOVE HIM AND OTHERS IN RE-TURN.

Yes, you are a unique and wonderful human being. You have a lot to offer. And you are loved.

Repeat this exercise every day for the next week. It can be the beginning point in a life of meaning . . . and deep down happiness.

Step number two is:

Continue the Process

Dr. Jeanne Segal says, "Life is a process and if we are not in the process of living, we are in the process of dying."

Now, I want to suggest five key areas which I hope you will explore and strengthen. They can significantly increase your happiness level.

1. *FIND A PURPOSE IN LIFE.* One that gives real meaning to your life. That can withstand the up's and down's—the tough times as well as the good times.

2. *DECIDE WHAT IS DEPENDABLE IN YOUR LIFE.* What can be counted on in the clutches to bring contentment, joy, and fulfillment? You must find this if you want to find happiness.

3. *TAKE RESPONSIBILITY FOR YOUR LIFE.* No one is ultimately responsible for your life but you. Be tough on yourself at this point. Take responsibility for your thoughts, words, actions, and attitudes. You cannot find lasting happiness without doing so.

4. *DEVELOP A WORKABLE WAY TO MOTIVATE YOURSELF.* One that will work when you're down, regardless of the obstacles.

5. *UNDERSTAND THAT LIFE REQUIRES CHANGE.* Life is never static. It is an ever-expanding exploration. You can kick and scream and be left behind. Or you can *grow*, moving your life in whatever direction you choose.

Remember Dr. Segal's statement, "Life is a process"? The dictionary defines "process" as "progress, advance . . . something going on . . . a natural unfolding marked by gradual changes that lead toward a particular result . . . a series of actions or operations leading to an end."

Since this is the case, you can't expect to instantly and perfectly put the above five points into action.

But you *can* begin.

The next chapter is designed to help you do this.

8

Self-Development

In this chapter I am providing a series of self-development exercises. Some of them you may want to do only once. Others you will want to repeat frequently. Each has but one purpose—helping you move toward contentment, fulfillment and happiness.

EXERCISE NO. 1
DEVELOPING AWARENESS

1. Get a sheet of paper on which to record your observations. Divide the page into three columns.

2. Over the first column write, "Activity." Over the second column, "Feelings." And over the third column, "Happiness Score."

3. At the end of the day, list in the first column all the things you can remember doing today, beginning from the moment you got up. Number each entry. List the decisions you made, the arguments you had, the

Joe R. Barnett

P. O. Box 100
Lubbock, Texas 79408

Dear Friend,

I am pleased to send your free copy of my new book, I Want To Be Happy. I'm glad you responded to our television program by asking for it.

And when I say your free copy I mean just that -- it's yours absolutely free.

What's the catch?

There is none. You will not be asked to pay for any materials we send -- and you'll not be asked for a donation. The television program -- and the book -- are being provided by people who genuinely care.

You are a very special person and we sincerely want to be your friend. No strings attached.

I hope you will read the book carefully -- and find it helpful.

Next month -- and most every month -- I'll be sending you a little booklet which I believe will help in your search for happiness.

Again, there is no charge.

Why do we do this?

Because we have found some answers which make life meaningful and happy. Not all the answers. We're still struggling. Searching. But we want to share what we have learned -- and are learning -- with you.

Just because we care.

Happily yours

Joe R. Barnett

P.S.   If I can be of personal help feel free to write.

circumstances which made you feel good, and the ones which made you feel bad. List the activities you engaged in. And the moments you spent thinking, planning or daydreaming. Everything you can think of.

4. When you have completed your list, return to the top of the page—and beside each entry in column 2, write how you feel NOW about that activity or incident. Happy. Sad. Guilty. Angry. Frustrated. Fulfilled. Whatever your feeling is.

5. Then return to the top of the page again. Look at each entry. If the activity, thought or event made you happy, place a plus (+) in column three beside that entry. If it didn't matter one way or another, place a zero (0) in the column. And if it brought unhappiness, place a minus (−) beside it.

Now you have an "awareness inventory" of yourself for one day. It's a tool for evaluation—and change.

Look back at the items beside which you placed a minus (−) mark.

Is there anything you could have done to have changed the "Happiness Score"?

—Could you have altered a person's action—or reaction—by a different attitude or approach?

—Could you have interpreted a person's actions differently—in other words, were you overly sensitive, wearing your feelings on your sleeve?

—Could you have used your time more productively? Could you have used your "down time"— while waiting in line, traffic, or for someone—to read, think, plan?

—Could you, by exercising a little self-discipline,
have come away from the minus experience with
a plus?

—Could you, by exercising a little positive-thinking, have neutralized a bad experience?

The list could go on. But I think you get the point.
Many of our minus experiences center in our own control—or lack of it. You can't control others, and you
can't always control circumstances. But it is amazing
how both are significantly altered by *self*-control. Controlling your *own* thoughts, actions, words and attitudes
can turn a lot of minuses into pluses in a hurry.

Repeat this exercise twice a week for the next
month. This will increase your awareness of what
makes you happy or unhappy. And it will provide a
method for tracking your success in changing the
things you want to change.

EXERCISE NO. 2
HANDLING STRESS

Stress is primarily a result of pressure and un-
avoidable disruptions in our lives. Since we live in a
fast-paced world, where it is increasingly difficult to
maintain a comfortable routine, we are having to learn
to live with more and more stress.

We need continuity or a quality of "sameness" to
keep us from self-destructing. Continuity provides our
"comfort zone"—an area where we can "let down." And
it's easy to fall into a pattern of depending on the wrong
kinds of things, such as overeating or watching too

much TV. It is a way of filling our hours, away from the arena which produces stress. But damaging and unproductive practices can produce side effects which create more problems than benefits.

Substitute new, helpful practices for old, unhealthy ones. You need comfortable and pleasant activities to release the pressures and stresses. But you should carefully choose practices that build up rather than tear down.

Here are some methods to help you:

*Instead of eating junk foods, choose healthy ones, even at snack time. Self-control is the name of the game. Control your food intake. Don't let it control you. You'll feel better. Look better. And your self-image will rise to new heights.

*Instead of watching a valueless television program, substitute an hour of exercise. Running, swimming, cycling, walking—any activity that gets you on your feet and outside. It is an excellent de-stressing activity.

*Instead of reading junk material, select a quality book which will add to your knowledge and personal development. Most self-help books contain useful information which will help you become more productive— and happy. And the Bible is an endless source of inspiration. (If you would like a guide for reading the Bible, just write me and I'll send you the one I use, without charge.)

*Instead of spending time with people who are negative and pessimistic, find those who are positive and fun to be with. Don't allow a chronic pessimist to keep you from growing. If he chooses to be a grouch that's his business. But you don't have to be poisoned by his gloomy disposition. Choose, instead, the company of those who build you up—who cause you to reach for the stars—who make you positive and happy.

EXERCISE NO. 3
BUILDING RELATIONSHIPS

A revealing discovery has been made in recent years by those who have made studies of persons who kill themselves while in jail.

We tend to think these kinds of tragedies involve persons overcome with remorse because of their crimes. Or persons sentenced to die being overwhelmed at the thought of execution.

That's not the case at all.

We now know that people who kill themselves while behind bars are usually young—an average age of 22. More often than not they have never been in jail before. And usually they have never tried to kill themselves before.

Most of those who commit suicide in jail are in isolation—for their own protection. And they have been there for only a short time, an average of just three hours. It is there, in isolation, that they die, victims of suicide.

Alone.

We know it helps *victims* of crime to have someone to talk with, someone to care. Even though crime always leaves its scars on its victims, those who have supportive friends, neighbors, relatives and family get over their emotional distress the quickest.

Not alone. Together.

When divorce destroys a marriage, previous investment in family relationships pays off. When other family members—children, parents and others—can be counted on to stand by, to sympathize, to listen and advise, the wound is less severe. For wives or husbands who have failed to make the investment of time and energy in the family relationship, the needed support usually isn't there. As one recently-divorced man lamented, "Just when I was ready to be with my family, I found I didn't have one."

Just when he wanted to experience "togetherness," he suffered "aloneness."

Traditionally, we have looked to the church to remind us that happiness must be anchored in reaching out and being reached out to. Now, modern medicine and modern psychology have reached the same conclusion. The need to belong.

Dr. Hans Selye, author of *Stress Without Distress,* was asked what he would say if he had to give one piece of advice to people about stress—about avoiding unhappiness. He answered: "I would offer the wisdom of the Bible translated into terms a scientist can easily accept today: 'Earn thy neighbor's love'."

Dr. Karl Menninger, of the famed Menninger Clinic in Kansas, once said, "Love cures people—both the ones who give it and the ones who receive it."

So here is both the most ancient and the most

modern prescription I know—*love cures.* It offers incredible possibilities for those who tap its reservoirs of strength and stamina.

Love cures, heals, and binds. Love soothes, repairs, and strengthens. Love encourages, blends, and mends.

Love keeps you from being alone.

The payoff makes love worth earning.

You need friends. Real friends. But they don't come from sitting around despondently wondering why people don't extend their friendship. They come from *being* a friend. When you become more concerned about *giving* friendship than *receiving* it, you are well on the way to having the friends you want.

So, take the offensive! Decide, beginning right now, you will *be* a friend.

Here's a place to begin.

In his little book, *Encounters With the Self,* Don E. Hamachek lists the qualities of people he believes make the best friends:

*They hold to their values and principles in the face of adverse opinion, although they are secure enough to change when in error.

*They are capable of acting on their own best judgment without feeling excessive guilt or regret if disapproved of by others.

*They do not spend undue time worrying about tomorrow or yesterday.

*They retain confidence in their ability to deal with problems, despite occasional failures and setbacks.

*They feel equally worthwhile to others as persons, neither superior nor inferior because of differences in ability or position.

*They are relatively relaxed in the presence of others, with an "I'm all right, you're all right" attitude.

*They can accept compliments and praise without false modesty.

*They tend to resist being dominated by others.

*They are able to accept a wide range of feelings within themselves and others, without the compulsion to act on every feeling.

*They are able to enjoy themselves in a wide variety of activities involving work, play, companionship or creative self-expression.

*They are sensitive to the needs of others.

*They tend to look for the best in others, believing most people are pretty decent despite their shortcomings.

Examine your own "friendship level" by evaluating how you measure up to these qualities. They give an admirable group of goals to shoot for. By improving in these areas, you can strengthen relationships which are important to you—and build new ones.

EXERCISE NO. 4
DEALING WITH PAIN

Occasionally, a human is born without the capacity to feel pain. That person is in jeopardy, because pain is an important signal that something is wrong and steps need to be taken to correct a problem.

The same is true of our mental and emotional hurts. The pain is a signal to make some corrections. As Jeanne Segal notes:

> As adults, we have choice, and within the context of choice, sadness and pain are experiences we can do something about. Painful feelings can guide us toward a more rewarding and fulfilling life. They teach us what not to do and they can also teach us about ourselves. In situations, for example, where we feel badly for no apparent reason we can ask why and follow the feelings to the source within us.

If you are hurting, answering the following questions may be helpful:

*Have I left something out of my life which has contributed to my pain?

*Is there something I am not allowing myself to see, acknowledge, or understand?

*Am I refusing to accept help in getting rid of the pain?

*Am I hurting because I am blaming myself for something I couldn't (can't) control?

*Am I hurting because I am refusing to face up to something, someone, or some need?

*Am I hurting because I have refused room in my life for something important?

Sure, there are times when we hurt from causes for which we have little responsibility and over which we have no control. But many of our hurts can be lessened by positive thinking and action. And no one can do that for you.

It's up to you.

PART THREE

Proven Paths

9

Happiness . . . A By-Product

When Leo Buscaglia, a professor of education at the University of Southern California, proposed a course in love, many of his teaching colleagues hooted. They poked a lot of not-so-humorous fun at him. Who ever heard of teaching "love" at a university?

But Buscaglia, a warm, witty, sensitive, *loving* man kept pressing. He wanted to teach that class. Why? Because in the winter of 1969, one of his students— beautiful, popular, bright, with excellent grades—drove her car out to the cliffs of Pacific Palisades. She parked—and plunged over the edge of a steep cliff, dying on the rocks below. She left behind no note of explanation. No hint of why she'd done it. Nothing.

Reflecting on her death, Buscaglia kept thinking of something Soren Kierkegaard once said: "To cheat oneself out of love is the most terrible deception; it is an eternal loss for which there is no reparation, either in time or in eternity."

While he couldn't teach the whole world about love, Dr. Buscaglia could explore the subject with one hundred students a year. And his class on love has grown into one of the most sought-after classes ever taught in an American University.

One of the mandatory requirements in Dr. Buscaglia's class is that each student do something for somebody.

One day a student named Joel asked, "What's there to do?"

"Joel, come with me," Buscaglia replied. Close to the university campus there is a nursing home, filled with old people lying around in cotton gowns, staring at the ceiling. Lonely and afraid. That's where Dr. Buscaglia took Joel.

"What'll I do here?" Joel asked. "I don't know anything about gerontology."

Buscaglia answered, "You see that lady over there? You go over and say hello."

"That's all?" Joel asked.

"That's all."

So Joel went over and said hello.

She looked at him suspiciously for a moment and then asked, "Are you a relative?"

He said he wasn't.

"Good!," she replied. "I hate my relatives. Sit down, son."

And they talked and talked. Joel kept going back. Soon the day that he made his weekly visit became known as "Joel's day." The women began having their hair done, and they dressed in their finest on "Joel's day."

One day, Dr. Buscaglia was walking across the campus when he noticed a strange sight—a group of about thirty elderly people shuffling down the sidewalk. And in front of the group was Joel, leading his friends to a USC football game. Dr. Buscaglia says seeing that scene was the greatest triumph in his educational career.

That's how Joel found happiness. Indirectly. He hadn't staked out a goal of *happiness* for himself. It wasn't an all-consuming, carefully mapped, tightly organized "search for happiness." But happiness is what he found.

This tells us something. Something important. Happiness is essentially a by-product. It comes by indirection. To pursue it, to pounce upon it, to go directly after it, is the surest way not to obtain it. Happiness is a "serendipity" (an agreeable thing not sought for), something added in the pursuit of something else. It's always a consequence—the "fruit" of good deeds. As the Bible puts it: "The *fruit* of the spirit is . . . *joy*" (Galatians 5:22).

To be sure, there are laws governing the search for happiness. For, while happiness comes indirectly, it does not come haphazardly. While it certainly is a "by-product," it doesn't come by accident. The achievement of happiness is based upon dependable laws. Fruits are inevitably related to roots, and consequences are traceable to causes.

If you fail to develop the capacity for happiness, you can't expect to possess it.

You can't find happiness if you don't know what to look for.

You can't have happiness if you are unwilling to yield to those things which produce it.

You can't be happy unless you honor the laws which give it birth.

So, let's look at the proven paths to happiness.

10

Where Happiness Is Found

For thousands of years, as we discussed in Chapter 5, people have sought happiness in pretty much the same ways—by pursuing possessions, popularity, pleasure, and power.

Likewise, for thousands of years people have *found* real happiness in pretty much the same ways. I'm not offering anything new here—just the consensus of history. Here is where happiness is found.

1. HAPPINESS IS FOUND IN SIMPLE THINGS

Reader's Digest recently carried the story of a man who spent an hour trying to rescue his young son's pet frog from the bottom of a narrow shaft. He used a long stick. He tried to "fish" the frog out using a rope with a loop at the end. And he tried some complicated procedures. Nothing worked, and he finally gave up.

Five minutes later his five-year-old son skipped through the front door, carrying his frog!

How had he done it?

Simple. As the *Digest* article explained, "The boy had hit on the idea of flooding the shaft with a garden hose and floating the frog to the surface."

It is often the simple things, the little things, the inexpensive and commonplace things that work best.

That's true with happiness, too.

The most popular film at the New York World's Fair in 1964 was entitled, "To Be Alive." Of the hundreds of films produced for the Fair, this one attracted the largest number of viewers. Interestingly, it had no plot. It was simply a series of unrelated scenes in the lives of average people. It showed a little Japanese boy rushing into a field of golden wheat. A young African boy rolling a hoop down a jungle trail. A grandfather, his face lined with wrinkles of age, and his eager grandson, fishing from a boat in a quiet pond. There were many scenes like that, focusing on the beauties and joys of simple things.

Norman Cousins, former editor of *Saturday Review* and now a senior lecturer at the School of Medicine at UCLA, tells what the simple act of sitting at the piano and playing did for Pablo Casals, the brilliant musician:

When I visited him a few years ago, he was terribly ill. Afflicted with arthritis, emphysema, and heart problems, he had to be helped downstairs every morning. But then he'd sit down at the piano, lower his crippled fingers over the keys, and miraculously his tendons would stretch out. Soon his fingers would be flying over the keyboard in a Bach fugue or a Brahms concerto. The color would return to his cheeks; his whole body would straighten. Energized, he'd march to the table for breakfast before taking a long walk on the beach. His body produced its own cortisone! Its own analgesic!

Cousins added, "Now not everyone is a Pablo Casals, with the ability to create beautiful sounds, but everyone has some creative ability which can stimulate the life juices if it's allowed expression."

In the last few pages, we've talked about a few "simple" things that have brought happiness to people. Talking with someone who is lonely. Taking 30 "senior citizens" to a college football game. Playing the piano. Watching a film with no plot. If you will just put a little of that "creative ability" that Norman Cousins spoke of to work, you can think of a hundred simple things that can make someone happy. And, in the process, you'll become happy too.

In fact, it may require nothing more than doing what you usually do—but just doing it in a different way.

Here are a few suggestions for doing simple, every-day things differently:

Include another person in something you usually do alone. Spend a lot of time at laundry? Then arrange to do your laundry with a neighbor who is lonely. Like to take walks? Ask someone who seems to need a friend to walk with you. You can add to the list can't you? Be creative.

Do something you enjoy. Like to read at night? Take a break—spend a whole afternoon reading. Or fishing. Or working in the garden or shop. Make it a special time—reflect, putter. Sample the happiness in simple things.

Talk about things you enjoy. If you enjoy cooking, call someone and share a favorite recipe. I'll bet she will be thrilled that you thought of her. You may say, "I don't know what to talk about. I don't know about anything but being a mother." Great! Then talk about being a mother. It's an important subject. And if you're not an expert, who is?

Do usual things in a different place. Do you always shop at the same place? Well, try something different for a change. A different supermarket or department store. Meet new people. Get new ideas. If you always walk or jog the same route, try a new one. Drink in the beauty of new surroundings. It's a big, beautiful world.

Rearrange your schedule. Are you in a rut—always doing the same things at the same time? Alter the schedule. Do something you want to do. Stop off at the public library. Treat yourself to dinner out. Take a picnic lunch to the park. Drive through a part of town you normally don't see. Break the monotony of your schedule. It may open up some exciting new horizons.

Advertise yourself. Not arrogantly. But force yourself to come out of the shell a bit. Smile—and give a cheerful "Hello" to people you meet. Leo Buscaglia, the professor who teaches the "love" class, does it all the time. He says people sometimes look puzzled, and ask,

"Do I know you?" And he answers "No, but wouldn't it be nice?"

Little things. But they make a difference. Use your own creativity. You can find a lot of happiness in simple things—things which cost nothing, but pay big dividends.

2. HAPPINESS IS FOUND IN WORTHWHILE WORK DONE WELL

Antoine de Saint-Exupery, the French writer, said, "It is using a pick-axe to no purpose that makes a prison."

No purpose! That's hard to live with.

Finding a cause larger than yourself is important. It energizes you. Gets you out of bed in the morning. Anxious to be up and going. It gives meaning to your life. It makes no difference whether others think your work is important, just as long as you do.

Look for the good. Be optimistic. Even if you have to force it at first. It's amazing how differently we "see" things. The pessimist looks at a half-filled glass and says, "It's half empty." The optimist says, "It's half full!"

George Moore wrote of Irish peasants who, during that country's Great Depression, were put to work building roads. They worked hard and sang their Irish songs with gusto. Happy to be working again. But then they discovered the roads they were building were leading nowhere. The work they were doing was just that—"make" work, with no purpose. The government had given them jobs just to keep them busy. They stopped singing. They lost heart. Moore said, "The roads to nowhere are difficult to make. For a man to work well and sing, there must be an end in view."

It is important to enjoy your work—something you can do only if you see its value. A medical doctor in Vienna once said, "There is nothing in the world which helps a man surmount his difficulties, survive his disasters, keep him healthy and happy, as the knowledge of a life task worthy of his devotion."

If you can't see any value in what you do for a living, you may want to think seriously about doing something different. You may want to consider going to night school to learn a new trade or develop new skills. You might consider an apprenticeship—signing on to learn a new way of earning a living.

Perhaps this isn't possible in your situation. And it may not be necessary. Maybe you just need to see your work differently. Like the half-filled glass—you may need to take a more optimistic view of what you do.

Here are some questions for you to think about in evaluating the worth of your work:

*Do you do it well; to the best of your ability?

*Do people depend on you? Even those who may not realize it? If you weren't there to do your job, would it create problems for others?

*Do you perform your job cheerfully? Are other people happier and more productive because you are there?

*When you leave for the day, do you feel good

about your performance? Have you done your best—
giving a full day's work for a day's pay?

*Have you considered what the ideal job would be
for you? How would that job differ from the one you
now have?

*What would you change about your present job to
make it more meaningful? Can that be done?

*How would it affect you to lose your present job?
If that happened, would you look back and view your
job differently?

I know there is a job shortage. But there is even a
greater shortage of people who appreciate their jobs,
and give them everything they have. People who throw
themselves into their work, always going the extra mile,
bring a lot of happiness to others—and to themselves.

I think of the elderly man who has a shoe shine
stand in the Nashville airport. I've never had a better
shine. He does it with the touch of an artist. And I
always leave whistling.

I think of the waitress who is always attentive and
cheerful.

The airline stewardess who is never surly. Even
when she encounters a rude, demanding passenger.

The secretary who makes you glad you called.

The chef who does it just right.

Hard jobs. Often dealing with difficult people. But
these, and thousands of others, make mundane jobs
sparkle. They do their work uncommonly well. And the
result? Happiness! For themselves, and others.

When I think of people who give 100% to their

work, I always think of two figures in professional sports.

One is Pete Rose. When most pro baseball players get a base on balls, they sluggishly trot to first base. Not Pete Rose. He *runs!* He also runs to and from his defensive position. He charges after foul balls as if they were base hits. He often slides headfirst when he runs the bases. What makes Pete run? "I have so much fun playing baseball," says Rose. "That's why I play the way I do."

Then there's Joe Namath, former pro-football quarterback. Joe played most of his pro career in great pain. Twice, he was awarded the Most Courageous Player award. One of Namath's rules for coping with pain is this: "If you've got a broken leg, go visit somebody who doesn't have a leg."

Happiness is found in meaningful work. And in doing our job to the very best of our ability.

3. HAPPINESS IS FOUND IN PURSUIT— NOT JUST ACHIEVEMENT

A form letter arrived in Hilton Gregory's mailbox one day. It was from the local historical society, pleading for volunteer researchers. Gregory describes what happened:

Within a week, I was on a study committee. Soon I was writing a paper, delivering a speech, meeting new friends. But the most remarkable thing is what the experience did

for my outlook and feelings. I found that my
spirit soared, borne aloft by the new interest.

At that point, Gregory hadn't really done much for
the society. But there was an excitement in being involved, being a part of something interesting and satis-
fying. He found happiness in the experience.

Satisfaction and happiness are often found more in
"doing" than in "having." In enjoying the trip as much
as arriving at the destination. It's not so much the
pursuit of happiness as it is the *happiness of pursuit.*

Happiness would be terribly short-lived if it came
only as an *end-result.* But it isn't that way. We find deep
happiness in the journey.

When we bring babies into the world we have an
end-result in view. We want them to reach adult life as
stable, well-trained, productive human beings. And we
are happy when that occurs. But, as we look back we
find some of our happiest moments were those spent
with our children at various stages of devlopment. The
journey—not just the destination.

Many a man has built a business empire. He had
goals. And achieved them. But he discovers that the real
happiness came in climbing those mountains, overcom-
ing obstacles. Happiness was more in the building process than in the final victory.

The trick is to understand this principle early. And
to decide to enjoy life at every phase—not to wait for
happiness, expecting it to suddenly come when all the
giants have been killed.

Jesus gave an overview of the happy life in his

Sermon on the Mount. He began the sermon with a list of "blesseds"—*nine ways to be happy.* Here is what he said:

> Blessed are the poor in spirit, for theirs is the kingdom of heaven.
> Blessed are those who mourn, for they shall be comforted.
> Blessed are the meek, for they shall inherit the earth.
> Blessed are those who hunger and thirst for righteousness, for they shall be satisfied.
> Blessed are the merciful, for they shall obtain mercy.
> Blessed are the pure in heart, for they shall see God.
> Blessed are the peacemakers, for they shall be called sons of God.
> Blessed are those who are persecuted for righteousness' sake, for theirs is the kingdom of heaven.
> Blessed are you when men revile you and persecute you and utter all kinds of evil against you falsely on my account.
>
> —*Matthew 5:3-11*

Isn't that amazing? How could such things bring happiness? Well, they provide the foundation for a lifestyle pointed in the right direction. Possessing these characteristics helps us approach the highest ideals for life. And the worth of an ideal is not measured by the degree to which we achieve it so much as by the direction it gives to life. We grow as we pursue—and that brings happiness.

Your life needs its dream, its goal, its seemingly unattainable ideals. Remember Alan Shepard, the first American in space? A decade passed before his second flight because of an inner ear problem.

He learned of a doctor whose operation might cure him. Checking into the hospital under an assumed name, he had the surgery and went through the gruelling training for a moon flight.

In February, 1971, Shepard, then 47 years old, stood on the moon. His wife watched on TV and said to reporters, "They can't call him Old Mose anymore. He's reached his promised land." He lived with a dream, devoted himself passionately to the process, and finally achieved it.

But what if he had never set foot on the moon? I strongly suspect Alan Shepard would still have said the struggle had been worth every sacrifice, every moment of hard work, every ounce of effort.

Alan Shepard had a goal. But it was achieved only because he devoted himself totally to the process. The journey. And that produces happiness.

Carl Rogers, the psychologist, said, "Real living, the kind of experience that transcends mere existence, always gets down to whether or not you're willing to take a chance. Regardless of your age, be it nine or ninety, a predictable lifestyle offers little opportunity for growth. The human potential is limitless, yet it can be restricted. Set up boundaries—past this point I am unwilling to venture—and how many horizons, how many doorways to increased knowledge slam shut forever?"

Yes, real happiness is achieved in diligent pursuit—not merely in having arrived.

4. HAPPINESS IS FOUND IN BEING "OTHERS"-CENTERED

When their son, Raun, was a year old, Barry and Suzi Kaufman noticed that he began to withdraw. Something was badly wrong. The doctors quickly diagnosed Raun as autistic, which is generally considered the most irreversible form of mental illness in children.

The Kaufmans sought out every medical authority they thought could shed any new light on their son's problem. They read dozens of books and hundreds of articles. Raun gave no signs of seeing anyone. He simply stared. Sometimes he would sit for hours and spin objects. Occasionally he would smile—but with no focus. He never spoke. He never pointed. He never cried. He never looked.

Many families give up on such children and put them in an institution. Others keep them, but only in caretaker roles. They don't know anything else to do, and are doing what they feel is best for the child. Raun's mother and father opted for a different strategy. They would enter Raun's world, being with him every waking hour, demanding nothing of him, reading to him, talking to him—simply accepting him and enjoying him as he was.

As Barry Kaufman would later describe in his book,

To Love Is To Be Happy With, this approach in dealing with their son brought enormous happiness to the Kaufman family. Their two daughters, Bryn, 8, and Thea, 5, soon joined the 24-hour therapy. The family was totally caught up in this outward-focus. There was no time for trivial matters.

Kaufman notes:

> Within eight months, this dysfunctioning, totally withdrawn, self-stimulating, functionally retarded and "hopeless" little boy became a social, highly verbal, affectionate and loving human being displaying intellectual capabilities precocious for his age . . . What we did was not the result of any special brilliance or capacity. Our energy and understanding was a product of our happiness and inner comfort with ourselves and our child. By clearing away fear and anxieties, we each create the opportunity to function more productively and more effectively.

The story of the Kaufman family illustrates how happiness is found more in being concerned about others than about self. When you invest yourself in bringing happiness to someone else, it has a way of coming back to you.

Now, let's make some observations, based on the attitude and actions of Suzi and Barry Kaufman, which will help as you seek to be others-centered:

In reaching out to others don't expect anything in return. If you do something for someone *expecting* a return on the investment, the act becomes selfish and disappointment is almost certain. People give you what they *want* to give. To *expect* more is putting conditions on your love. And that is a sure road to unhappiness.

Be patient. Meaningful relationships must have time and room to grow. People are different. We grow at our own rate, in our own way, in our own time. If you act in genuine love and concern . . . you wait.

Giving happiness to others is an adventure. Expect it to bring new discoveries about others—and about yourself. Be patient—but be active. Take care not to force your expectations and demands on others. But be alert, doing all you can to open new doors, new opportunities. It will be a "discovery" process—finding what works and what doesn't. And you will grow in the process.

Express yourself, understanding that you are running the risk of being rejected. You must make the first move. This requires courage—the courage to make a mistake, to suggest something that doesn't work out. And the courage to share down's as well as up's.

The beauty of it is that as you make these moves, not only do you bring happiness to others, but also that a New You begins to emerge. The loneliness which may have plagued you in the past begins to evaporate. You may have felt almost invisible. No one knew you were there. Know the feeling?

But if you begin to reach out to give happiness to

others, your real "self" begins to fill in. The fog lifts. And there is a New You for the world to contend with.

The "frog" you felt yourself to be suddenly becomes a prince or a princess!

The wonderful, beautiful, important, valuable "you" is no longer invisible. And it's really so simple. It is only a matter of being alert to others—of being unselfish and sharing.

The late Dr. Batsell Barrett Baxter told about an illustration used by the speaker at his college graduation. A lady in his church baked a chocolate cake for his family and brought it to the church office. He set the cake on a table beside a window.

After awhile he noticed several boys from the not-too-well-to-do neighborhood had stopped their games and were looking through the window at the cake. On impulse, he invited them in and shared the cake with them. It was soon gone, but the warm memory of that happy group of boys never left him. He told that graduating class months later that he was still enjoying that cake. Dr. Baxter said, "And a generation later, I'm still enjoying a cake which I never saw or tasted."

And now that you've read this story, *you* are enjoying a cake you never saw or tasted. How different the story would be if that man had kept the cake only for himself.

It doesn't require great, heroic, headline deeds. Just little things—things which show your interest and concern for others. But it pays handsome happiness dividends.

For them, and for you.

5. HAPPINESS IS FOUND IN THE SPIRITUAL DIMENSION

In the 1960s and early '70s in the United States, the church got a lot of bad press. In their search for happiness many people eliminated the spiritual dimension as outdated. The "Me" generation emerged, talking about looking out for No. 1, and doing your own thing. Many felt that psychology had more answers than religion.

But the pendulum didn't stay anchored very long in the camp of the "Me" generation. Recently, Connecticut Mutual Life Insurance Company conducted a poll and found that 74 percent of the American people say they are religious. Seventy-three percent feel God loves them. And about 50 percent frequently pray or go to services of worship. In fact, 45 million Americans say they are "intensely religious."

I'm not surprised.

We are more than animals. There is a spiritual side of us, and one of the clear lessons of history is that happiness doesn't exist until we deal with that dimension.

Our lives have been lived in a time of knowledge explosion. Yet, men keep returning to ancient truths to find how to live happily. We keep returning to those truths for peace and contentment. "Great peace have those who love thy law; nothing can make them stumble," said the Psalmist.

Without that peace, we churn inside. We toss and turn. We can't sleep without counting sheep—or swallowing pills. *With* that peace, we have "wholeness," completeness—the *happiness* Solomon talked about when he said fearing God and keeping his commandments is the "whole of man."

How do we find a meaningful relationship with God, the kind that will stay with us through good and through bad, in sickness and health?

In short, "How do we find God?"

It's not a new question. Eight centuries before Christ, Israel's prophets had a hard time getting people to accept God because he wasn't the kind of God they expected. Neighboring nations had gods that were touchable—idols made of metal, wood, or stone. But this "Jehovah" the prophets talked about was so distant. They couldn't see him. Or touch him. So they rejected him and turned to idols.

You see, it isn't just the non-religious who reject God. Often it is the very religious, whose preconceived notions force God to fit their mold—or else.

When God came into the world in the form of a baby in Bethlehem's stable, it just didn't measure up to people's expectations. They were expecting a king, wearing regal robes. Instead they got a baby, wrapped in swaddling clothes.

And where was his sword? They had the boot of foreign oppression on their neck. They expected the Messiah to deliver them. Instead of a sword he came with a basin of water and a towel. Not a warrior, but a servant.

They expected *Jesus Christ, Superstar*—this "gentle Jesus, meek and mild" would never do.

But, "God's ways are not our ways." God knew what

he was doing. This was the only way. God, in Jesus, became like us. He knew we'd have trouble identifying with someone who seemed so far away and so different from us. So he became like us.

No metal, wood, or stone. But flesh and blood.
He experienced the same life-cycle:
> birth,
> infancy,
> childhood,
> adolescence,
> just like us.

He got hungry
> thirsty,
> tired,
> lonely,
> just like us.

He faced the same temptations we face. He put himself in our shoes. And people found him approachable. Tax collectors, prostitutes, soldiers, religious leaders. They found him to be a friend. He was even called a friend of sinners. And he was that.

Toward the end of his life he said, "Greater love has no man than this, that a man lay down his life for his friends." And then he did that—laid down his life for us. All of us—
> rich,
> poor,
> educated,
> uneducated,
> all of us.

It was God's way of bridging the gap.

Jesus said, "Come to me, all who labor and are heavy laden, and I will give you rest. Take my yoke upon you, and learn from me; for I am gentle and lowly in heart, and you will find rest for your souls" (Matthew 11:28,29).

I don't want to preach at you. Especially if you're not ready for that. But I can't honestly tell you how to find happiness without talking about the spiritual side. Happiness is the by-product of holiness. If that sounds too "theological," then say happiness is the by-product of wholeness. It's the same thing: health, wholeness, holiness—all of these words have the same root.

The complexity—and richness—of the human personality is its variety—physical, mental, moral, spiritual. When we ignore the "wholeness" of our nature, concentrating only on a fragment, trying to satisfy one part of us at the expense of the rest of us, we end up with temporary pleasures. But not happiness.

That's why those who seek happiness only in sensual pursuits are always disappointed. They are leaving the rest of themselves unfulfilled. It's like feeding the mind and starving the body. Soon there is deterioration. And death.

Jesus understood this. He came that you might have life—and have it abundantly. When you move in that direction the result is happiness—happiness which can survive any kind of circumstances.

11

It's Your Turn

Now, it's your turn!
Throughout this book I have repeatedly
pointed out two things:

First, changing life is a *process.* It doesn't happen
all at once. It's a matter of small victories, one step at a
time.

Second, you have to *begin.* Take that first step. And
that is what I want to ask you to do now.

For the next five days select one of the following
"Today" resolutions and fulfill it. If you feel uncomfort-
able with one of them, skip it for the present, and come
back to it later. Repeat one of the others in its place.

Then, next week, do the same exercise again. Continue repeating the process each week until it becomes
habit. *And watch the new, wonderful you emerge.*

I've based this action list on the principles in chapter ten. Go back and review the chapter as you put
these resolutions into action.

Here is the list:

TODAY RESOLUTIONS

*TODAY I will notice and enjoy some simple pleasure in life which I have been taking for granted.

*TODAY I will find something worthwhile and fulfilling in my work. I will not perform my job slovenly or grudgingly, but will do it to the very best of my ability.

*TODAY I will enjoy life, rather than looking forward to happiness in the distant future.

*TODAY I will think of others rather than only myself. I will do something for another without expectation of thanks or reward.

*TODAY I will nurture the spiritual dimension. I will take time to read from the Bible, to pray, and to reflect on my relationship with God.

When Darrell Porter, the St. Louis Cardinal catcher, walked out of the drug and alcohol treatment center in 1980, he was given a small medallion which had Reinhold Niebuhr's "Serenity Prayer" inscribed on it. I urge you to make it your prayer:

God grant me the serenity
To accept the things I cannot change,

Courage to change the things I can,
And wisdom to know the difference.

Best wishes—and God bless you.